PLEASE REMIND ME HOW FAR I'VE COME

Theresa

Keep on keeping on!

[signature]

Heb 6:3

BOOKS IN THE **LIFELINES FOR RECOVERY** SERIES

Zondervan's **Lifelines for Recovery** series emphasizes healthy, step-by-step approaches for dealing with specific critical issues.

PLEASE REMIND ME HOW FAR I'VE COME

REFLECTIONS FOR CODEPENDENTS

JAN SILVIOUS · CAROLYN CAPP

Zondervan Publishing House
Grand Rapids, Michigan

Please Remind Me How Far I've Come
Copyright © 1990 by Jan Silvious and Carolyn Capp

This is a Daybreak Book
Published by the Zondervan Publishing House
1415 Lake Drive, S.E., Grand Rapids, Michigan 49506

Library of Congress Cataloging-in-Publication Data

Silvious, Jan, 1944–
    Please remind me how far I've come : reflections for codependents /
Jan Silvious, Carolyn Capp.
      p. cm.
    ISBN 0-310-34341-0
    1. Codependents—Prayer—books and devotions—English. I. Capp,
Carolyn. II. Title.
    BV4596.C57S54   1990
    242'.66—dc20   90–33912
                                                             CIP

All Scripture quotations, unless otherwise noted, are taken from the HOLY BIBLE:
NEW INTERNATIONAL VERSION (North American Edition). Copyright © 1973,
1978, 1984, by the International Bible Society. Used by permission of Zondervan
Bible Publishers.

Printed in the United States of America

90 91 92 93 94 95 / CH / 10 9 8 7 6 5 4 3 2 1

*To the rare and wonderful
group of people who have
come alongside of us
in each decade of our lives.*

*You know who you are,
for we have called
each of you "friend."
We're grateful ... We love you.*

Jan Silvious and Carolyn Capp

CODEPENDENCY

Codependency is a relationship between two people who allow one another's behavior to affect profoundly each other. In an attempt to "feel good" about himself/herself, one will try to control the physical, emotional, and spiritual well-being of the other for the sake of himself/herself.

CONTENTS

Overcoming....

ACKNOWLEDGMENTS

An author is lost without a support team ... mine keeps me going and keeps me straight!

Thanks, Guys. . . .

Thanks, Mom and Dad. . . .

I love you,
—Jan

With love and appreciation to my family, John, Johnny, Linda, Gary, and Brad. . . .

and to my special friend, Scott. . .

and my special friend, Renee. . .

who have been great encouragers in my first venture as an author! Thanks!

—Carolyn

With gratitude to Nia Jones, our editor, for her patience and belief in this book. It's been a pleasure.

DEAR FRIEND,

Grief is never easy to bear. That's a fact. The pain of losing a relationship and having to change in order to find emotional wholeness is difficult to reconcile. To go back to the old, familiar behaviors is comfortable, but defeating. To keep on with recovery is uncomfortable, but rewarding. So, many times in the process, you will find yourself suspended between the two. Desiring to go on, you will long to go back. The feelings can be overwhelming, sometimes even frightening.

For this reason, we have written this book. It is for you to remember how far you've come and to reflect on the goodness of God, no matter how you are feeling. It will also give you a special place to keep a record of your personal progress and your relationship with the Lord. You will find yourself returning to these pages over and over to be reminded of the long way you have come and of how much your Lord cares.

You will get better. In fact, you will be healed, but remember that it will take time.

We are praying for you and loving you from afar,

Jan Silvious

and

Carolyn Cyr

CONFUSION

For a while, it seemed that the situation was beginning to take on some semblance of order. The issues had been discussed and agreement had seemed to be reached. But now, the relationship is in a swirl again.

There are some misunderstandings. The expectations you thought were long gone have resurfaced. The hurts you thought were healed are smarting again. The question keeps coming back, "Will this situation never be settled?"

In your heart of hearts, you allow yourself the luxury of musing about the first days of the relationship. You ask yourself, "Wouldn't it be wonderful if the early days could be frozen in time, if the simplicity of meeting, enjoying, communicating, appreciating could be continued ... untainted by infatuation, disappointment, arguments, accusations, tears and pain?" But, the present comes rushing in, demanding your attention. And, with it, confusion reigns.

There is One who will allow you time to remember and the wisdom to move on. Why not turn to Him?

O Father, I don't know what to do. My life is changing ... I feel so unsettled. Which way should I go? What is best? How can I know? There is no one to ask, no one who knows the me deep down inside.

I turn to You ... and then I remember ...

You have always known me ...
You search my heart ... You know my every thought ...
You will work in me to want to do Your will ...
You will show me great and mighty things when I call on You ...
You will say to me, "This is the way, walk ye in it. ..."
You love me ... You care ...
You know what I should do ... You will lead me.

Thank you for knowing me and loving me. Thank you for caring what happens to me ... for listening to me ... for showing me what to do. Thank you that I can trust You with all my life. . . .

"I am the Lord your God, who teaches you what is best for you, who directs you in the way you should go."

(Isaiah 48:17)

"For it is God who works in you to will and to act according to his good purpose."

(Philippians 2:13)

REFLECTIONS

DISCORD

It really smarts to read what God says about quarrels. In fact, you would rather not read it, but there it is. "What is causing the quarrels and fights among you? Isn't it because there is a whole army of evil desires within you? You want what you don't have, so you kill to get it" (James 4:1–2).

You know what you want. You just want "the other" to exercise some responsibility for his behavior. But somehow that strains the relationship. You bring up a problem and instead of discussing it like rational human beings, you find yourselves jousting with one another. You take aim with your words to make your point and just as you think you have hit the target, your breath is taken away. "The other" has managed to score a near-fatal blow with a poisonous barrage of words. You crawl away to recuperate but you know this can't be the end. The quarrels will be stopped. But you just can't seem to find a way to break the cycle. Soon, before either of you suspect a quarrel is about to erupt, you find yourself locked in combat.

There is only One who can step between the two of you and stop the carnage of your spirits and your relationship. Why not turn to Him?

O Father ... how could a relationship that seemed so right in the beginning become so edgy ... so tense ... so guarded? If we really are as close as we say ... if we truly do love as You would have us love ... why so many quarrels? The weight of the friction is heavy. The walls between us are built on defensiveness and pride ... they are self-seeking. I feel frustrated ... irritated ... controlled. I don't like it this way, but it goes on ... and on ... and on.

We quarrel over feeling left out ... over being insensitive or too sensitive ... over not enough attention or too much attention ... over what we said wrong or didn't say ... over what should have been done differently.

Where is the peace? Where is the comfort? Where is the love You said we should have for one another?

"Let love be without hypocrisy. Abhor what is evil; cling to what is good. Be devoted to one another in brotherly love; give preference to one another in honor...."

(Romans 12:9–10 NASB)

O God, make me like that. Whatever You must do in my life ... in my relationships ... show me how to love the way You love ... without hypocrisy. Teach me to hate evil and to cling to what is right.

Teach me Your truths about brotherly love ... about putting others first. Teach me to be sensitive to Your Spirit ... that others might be able to see Your character in me ... and walk in peace.

REFLECTIONS

DISTRESS

The pressure on your chest feels like an elephant. It's like a heart attack . . . but you know it is only pressure that just won't go away. Stress, distress, heaviness, pain . . . stones piled on your chest, pushing on your heart . . . and you feel as though you'll never be free of the pain again.

When you go to sleep, your dreams are filled with scenes you long for, scenes of happiness, of love, and acceptance that suddenly turn into scenes of strife and arguing. The change is so abrupt. You awake with a start. Your heart pounds. Your head throbs. Then you realize it was all a dream . . . the good and the bad. Baffled by what it all means, you try to go back to sleep. Somehow trying doesn't get you there.

When sleep doesn't come, take time to talk with your heavenly Father. You can be sure He's awake.

O God, sometimes I feel as if I am falling apart . . . I am losing ground. My heart cries out . . . but no one hears my cries . . . no one sees my tears . . . no one knows that I am crumbling.

Then, faintly . . . in muffled tones of care and understanding . . . I hear Your words of comfort. . . .

"Come to me, all you who are weary and burdened, and I will give you rest."

(Matthew 11:28)

"Do not be anxious about anything, but in everything, by prayer and petition, with thanksgiving, present your requests to God."

(Philippians 4:6)

I listen. Your words fill my mind. They become clear and intense. You are speaking to me . . . to the very heart of me.

I am weary . . . I am burdened . . . my spirit needs rest.

I will come to You. I will not be anxious any longer . . . I will pour out my soul to You, with thanksgiving for Your drawing me to Yourself . . . for Your everlasting faithfulness to me. I will leave my neediness with You because I can trust You. I will have Your peace.

"And the peace of God, which transcends all understanding, will guard your hearts and your minds in Christ Jesus."
(Philippians 4:7)

REFLECTIONS

_____

_____

_____

_____

_____

_____

_____

_____

_____

_____

_____

_____

WORRY

So many "what if's" circulate through your mind. Insecurity about the future staggers you. You don't want to worry. You want to be pleasing to God, to stop being anxious, to trust Him in everything, but you have to be honest with yourself. You can trust Him with so much ... until it comes to this relationship.

You know it is on shaky ground. It has always been shaky and very reminiscent of the house built on sand. The winds have blown and the rains have come down and something is going to have to change, because the house is falling, falling, falling. Of course, it hasn't totally fallen yet, but there are no guarantees. And right now, you need guarantees. You need the assurance that if you become healthy, assume responsibility for your emotions and embark on a course of wholeness with God and man, you will still have "the other" or some "other" around to care for you, to be cared for.

And that's worrisome because you have never persistently pursued rightness with God and man. You have wanted to, but it always seemed risky. Well, now you know it really is risky, and that worries you. But there is one reassuring thing to hang on to. God loves you, cares for you and knows all about yesterday, today and tomorrow ... but He isn't worried.

Lord, I know the relationship which is so dear to my heart is not what You want it to be ... You have clearly shown me. Your Spirit convicts my spirit ... Your Word speaks Your truth and shows me my err. I know that I follow too closely ... I am too dependent ... I grasp and cling to someone other than You. I am wrong.

But, Father, I worry about being different ... even in becoming who You want me to be. What if I change and he doesn't understand? What if he likes me the way I am now? What if he gets angry with me ... turns against me ... walks away? What if he finds someone else? What will I do if I am left alone?

I agonize over these questions ... but I can't know the answers. I am weary of worrying. I have decided to trust You ... to obey You.

Your Word teaches me that ... You are for me (Psalm 56:9), You are in control of what happens to me (Daniel 4:35).

You tell me not to be anxious, but to ... Pray (Philippians 4:6), tell you exactly what I want (Philippians 6), and commit my relationships and my circumstances to you (1 Peter 2:24).

Thank you, Father, that You have not left me alone to worry ... to wonder ... to be torn between my heart's desire to be the person You created me to be and my fears of what might happen if I change. Thank you that You have provided a way for me. Thank you for loving me ... just because You want to love me.

REFLECTIONS

_____

_____

_____

_____

_____

_____

_____

_____

_____

HOPELESSNESS

You've heard it said over and over. "The one element man needs to survive is 'hope'." It's frightening to you that your survival depends on an emotion that is so non-existent in your life. Hope. What a strange four-letter word. You reach for it but it eludes your grasp. You long for it, pray for it, think you almost have it, then you remember that you have been disappointed so many times. Why should you hope?

You have reached the point that you know you have to hope ... or admit defeat. But from somewhere deep within, the question rises. "What am I hoping for?"

Are you hoping for security, for a place to belong, for love that won't disappear, for an identity? Is that too much to ask?

"The other" says you want too much, more than anyone can give. Is it really too much to expect? Why do some seem to have it? Why do some act so together, so secure? Why is security so hopelessly illusive for you?

God knows your heart. He hears your questions. He invites you to come to Him ... and He promises He will give you a place to belong, a love that won't disappear and an identity that can never be shaken. He promises a future ... and more than that, He promises hope.

O Father, deep inside my heart, the will to carry on fades. I feel alone ... isolated ... separated from the warmth of love and acceptance of one once so close. I am lonely ... so lonely.

Yesterday ... was it only yesterday ... I felt so secure ... so sure of who I was. I believed I was loved ... I rested in the loyalty of a dedicated friend. We shared every part of our lives and I believed we would always be there for each other. We were together in thought and heart, if not in actuality ... and I felt like somebody special. Today ... it's over. We have each gone our separate ways. The reasons are so complex ... so deep. Who can understand?

O God, I hear Your voice. You are speaking to me. You are calm and kind ... and so very gentle. The sound of Your voice reminds me that You love me ... that You understand ... that You are there for me. I feel Your arms around me ... You are holding me close to Your heart.

I see a glow of light at the end of my dark tunnel ... I have a glimmer of hope. As I keep my eyes on You ... as I remember who You are ... as I rest in You ... the light becomes brighter and my hope grows bigger and bigger. I believe I can go on ...

I have decided to trust You with me ... with my relationships, with my understanding, and with who I am. I will trust You with the healing of my heart. I am ready to begin again ...

"He heals the brokenhearted. And binds up their wounds."
(Psalm 147:3)

"For I know the plans I have for you," declares the Lord, "plans to prosper you and not to harm you, plans to give you hope and a future."
(Jeremiah 29:11)

REFLECTIONS

_____

_____

_____

_____

_____

_____

TRIALS

You never dreamed that the trial of your faith would be played out on the stage of this relationship. You never dreamed that you would be tested in the one area of your life that had given you such comfort.

Now here it is ... and you are torn by the agony of obeying God at all costs.

Your eyes have been opened. You see how you have chosen over and over to disobey God just to please "the other." You have given in to pleading, to cajoling, to manipulation. You have given in to do the very thing you never thought you would do.

Now you have clearly seen your behavior as sin. It has been a slow process for you to realize that trying to please someone else can really be wrong. You have come to understand that when pleasing "the other" defies God's rules, then you have gone too far. You never thought you would go too far, but you did. Now here you are in an arena you never expected to enter. Other people had to make life-changing decisions that would change their world forever, but not you...

When the stress seems too great to bear, take your questions, your hurts, your misgivings to your Heavenly Father...

O Father ... this trial is too great for me. I don't know what to do ... I see no way out ... no light at the end of the tunnel. No hope.

At times like this, I almost wonder if You know ... or care ... but then I remember these two Truths: Your plans for me are for a future and a hope ... and I can ask You for wisdom about anything.

Thank you for Your Truths. Thank you for hope. Thank you that I can come to You for wisdom ... that You long to give it to me generously and without reproach ... that Your ways are always perfect.

I will wait for Your answer. I will neither lean on my own understanding nor trust only in the advice of friends, even though they mean well. I will listen to You, for I know Your wisdom is pure, peaceable, gentle, reasonable, full of mercy and good fruits, unwavering and without hypocrisy.

"Let the morning bring me word of your unfailing love, for I have put my trust in you. Show me the way I should go, for to you I lift up my soul."

(Psalm 143:8)

"And we know that in all things God works for the good of those who love him, who have been called according to his purpose."

(Romans 8:28)

REFLECTIONS

A BROKEN RELATIONSHIP

You never have been a quitter. In fact, in your vocabulary, "quit" and "fail" are equal. But now, the course you never wanted to pursue has been completed. You made a choice. You broke the relationship you once held so dear. At times the bond felt like marriage.

You can't believe that you were actually the one to say, "No more." A few years ago you would have said, "Impossible . . . there's no way I'll ever break away." But, now you've done it because it is right . . . because the unrighteousness finally became too evident to ignore. You didn't want to be the one to take a stand. But, in your heart of hearts, you knew the ongoing pain, turmoil, quarreling and abuse had to stop. The only question was, "When?"

Well, "when" is now . . . and your heart feels shredded by the turbulent winds of change. But there is someone, only One, who can be your anchor.

O Lord . . . sometimes the pain seems unbearable. . .

It's ending it all that hurts. It's knowing that it's over. It's death to a part of my life.

It's not being able to make it right. . .

The pain is deep and sharp . . . almost overwhelming. I feel crushed . . . shattered . . . used . . . deceived. Every thought and every emotion screams at me.

But, Father, even in the midst of all this . . . even now . . . even here . . . even to me . . . You still say that You have plans for my life . . . to prosper me and not to harm me . . . plans for a future and a hope (Jeremiah 29:11). You say that You are working all things together for good in my life (Romans 8:28). I know that You are in control because You do as You please with the powers of heaven and the peoples of the earth. No one can hold back Your hand or say to You: "What have you done?" (Daniel 4:35). Thank you for Your promises of hope.

I pray that You will use this trial to make me more like Jesus . . . that my suffering will teach me to be more sensitive, more understanding, more caring and more compassionate to others who suffer. I ask You for wisdom that I might be wiser in my relationships in the future. Thank you for loving me and for teaching me . . . for being close to me when I hurt.

"When you pass through the waters, I will be with you; and when you pass through the rivers, they will not sweep over you. When you walk through the fire, you will not be burned; the flames will not set you ablaze. For I am the Lord, your God, the Holy One of Israel, your Savior. . . ."

(Isaiah 43:2–3)

"He sent forth his word and healed them; he rescued them from the grave."

(Psalm 107:20)

REFLECTIONS

FAILURE

You are haunted with the fear that you will fail. When you try to make things right, to talk things over, to express your feelings, something goes wrong.

You try to live up to your own standard of what is good and right, but it never seems to be enough to satisfy the one who seems to still have such a hold on the way you feel.

You even feel like a failure in assuming responsibility for your own emotions. Finding out you can control your feelings was a big step for you. It felt like success when you first realized you had the power to take charge of how you feel. Now, something has gone wrong and it feels like failure. You have let your guard down and your tender, healing emotions have been wounded. You have been assured these feelings are normal when you go through such dramatic change. Old emotions die hard but you really expected not to have such strong feelings. In many ways your feelings of failure are a surprise "especially when I was doing so well."

God knows your frailty. He knows your heart. He would never call you a failure. It would never cross His mind.

Lord, sometimes I feel like such a failure ... beaten down. So many broken promises ... broken plans ... broken relationships ... unfulfilled dreams ... disappointment upon disappointment ...

I come to You...

You say I can be victorious ... always ...
  In my spirit...
    In my soul...
      In my mind.
Anywhere I go ... anything I do...
  Because You will be with me and strengthen me...

I am to walk with courage and to obey all that You
    say...
I am to keep my thoughts on You ... on Your Word...
I am not to become discouraged or fearful.

For You are with me to strengthen me for my journey.

Then I will have peace...
Then I will have courage...
Then I will have victory.

"Those who hope in the Lord will renew their strength. They will soar on wings like eagles; they will run and not grow weary, they will walk and not be faint."

(Isaiah 40:31)

"Thou wilt keep him in perfect peace, whose mind is stayed on thee; because he trusteth in thee."

(Isaiah 26:3 KJV)

REFLECTIONS

_____

_____

_____

_____

_____

_____

_____

_____

_____

_____

ANGER

You feel the pressure inside. The rage is intense. It leaves you with an unreasonable set to your jaw. It brings an outrageous look to your eye. You hate the sharpness you hear in your voice and the fast-moving movie that plays in your mind. "The other's" wrongs race by in unceasing succession. Events you had forgotten become the main scenes. And, with each unfolding memory, the anger in you burns.

You see yourself as the fool. "The other" waltzes off with all the benefits. Others see you and wonder. Were you the one who caused the problem? You know the truth, but why try to explain? With each unfolding memory, the anger burns deeper.

There is One who understands your anger. He knows the truth and His name is Jesus Christ.

O God, I am angry. The feeling is intense... though the anger mingles with hurt and confuses me. The lines are blurred ... the emotions are muddled ... but both hurt and anger are there ... they run deep. I feel manipulated by deceit which came as subtly as the serpent... it controlled, it divided ... and it enraged. I am disappointed... I feel used. I believed ... I trusted ... I cared ... but, I was wrong.

Father, I know that I cannot allow resentment to grow. I must get up and go on. I must begin again ... Your way.

As I confront this bitter testing, I must remember what You have taught me...

... to not be overcome with evil, but overcome evil with good.

(Romans 12:21)

... to give a gentle answer to turn away wrath ... a harsh word stirs up anger.

(Proverbs 15:1)

... to replace my anger with forgiveness, just as you have forgiven me.

(Ephesians 4:32)

... to follow the example of Jesus who did not retaliate, but committed Himself to you who judges righteously.

(1 Peter 2:21–24)

Thank you for understanding how I feel . . . for giving me a way to handle this anger. Thank you that You have provided a way for me to have peace of mind . . . to regain the joy which escaped me. Thank you that I can have Your peace simply by choosing to do what You say . . . and that You will empower me to do it.

REFLECTIONS

BITTERNESS

It is hard to believe that someone you loved so much, someone you trusted, could have hurt you so much. It wasn't the careless little things that spread the seeds of bitterness. Those are easy to forgive when you love someone. But, what do you do with the obvious, big hurts that seem so pre-meditated, so pointed, so painful?

The surprise now is the bitterness you feel. You never expected to feel that way, no matter how much you were hurt. But, one day it was as if something snapped. You crossed over an imaginary line and bitterness met you head on. It surrounded you and filled you, and then you became the very thing you thought you would never be ... a bitter person.

You hate it. You don't want it, but the struggle to be rid of it is mighty.

Tell the Father who loves you. His love for you is never affected by the way you feel ... it is always steadfast and unmovable because you are His.

O Father, I hate the way bitterness feels. It closes in on me before I see it coming ... before I feel its presence ... before I pinpoint it's name. It consumes my thoughts ... it controls my feelings ... it eats away at my heart. What can stand against it, O God? What can defeat its power over me?

"For if you forgive men when they sin against you, your heavenly Father will also forgive you. But if you do not forgive men their sins, your Father will not forgive your sins."

(Matthew 6:14–15)

"Bear with each other and forgive whatever grievances you may have against one another. Forgive as the Lord forgave you."

(Colossians 3:13)

"Be kind and compassionate to one another, forgiving each other, just as in Christ God forgave you."

(Ephesians 4:32)

Forgiveness, choosing not to hold a grudge, letting go of a wrong commitment, is a characteristic of Jesus Christ who responds in love rather than in anger. God has purposed to make me like Jesus, to conform me to His image. To be like Him, I must forgive.

Father, I am willing for You to so work in my heart that I will think and behave in a way which reflects Jesus. Thank you that You are the great Enabler . . . that You will enable me to forgive . . . to overcome bitterness by letting go of the wrong done to me.

"See to it that no one comes short of the grace of God; that no root of bitterness springing up causes trouble, and by it many be defiled. . . ."

(Hebrews 12:15)

REFLECTIONS

_____

_____

_____

_____

_____

_____

_____

GRIEF

"The other" is not dead, but the feelings of emptiness, of loss, are as great as if he had been suddenly, tragically taken away.

In your heart, you know that you miss the routine more than anything. You miss picking up the phone just to talk. You miss the spontaneous get-togethers. You even miss the conflict. Isn't that strange? The conflict was a connection with reality that let you know the relationship existed. Even though it was battered, bruised and finally mortally wounded, at least for a while it lived. And, haven't you heard that "Where there's life there if hope"?

Now the life is gone. "The other" has chosen to go a different direction and the smell of burning bridges is a reminder that can't be denied. "What was" no longer exists. "What is" has become its own reality. For you, grief is ever present and must be worked through.

It is never easy to grieve. God knows that and is there to walk you through the valley of the shadow . . . to lighten your path and to see you through to the other side.

It's winter in my mind. I feel as one sitting in the shadows, chilled and still. I feel a sense of sadness . . . grief . . . as though there has been a death. I seek Your healing, but there are times I am almost overwhelmed by these feelings.

Why do I grieve? You show me the loss in my life . . . the death . . . and it helps me understand.

There has been death. . .
* To a close relationship with one I love. . .*
* To hopes and dreams of being together. . .*
* To security in knowing someone would always be*
*   there. . .*

But, Father, I know that I do not have to be swallowed up by this grief. You are my comforter . . . the one who restores my soul. Thank you that You are touched by whatever touches me . . . that You, too, have grieved . . . that You understand my grief. Thank you for Your Word which says. . .

"Now may our Lord Jesus Christ Himself and God our Father, who has loved us and given us eternal comfort and good hope by grace, comfort and strengthen your hearts in every good work and word."

(2 Thessalonians 2:16–17 NASB)

" 'Because he loves me,' says the Lord, 'I will rescue him; I will protect him, for he acknowledges my name. He will call upon me, and I will answer him; I will be with him in trouble, I will deliver him and honor him.' "

(Psalm 91:14–15)

I pray that I will honor You in word and deed as I go through this time of mourning. I will take one day at a time. I will fill my mind with Your Word . . . who You are, my relationship with You, Your will and Your ways. I will draw near to You and abide in You . . . that those who are watching might know that You are sufficient to sustain me and that You will continue the work You have begun in me.

REFLECTIONS

REJECTION

You never meant for things to end this way. All along you dreamed that someday the problems would be settled and you would know beyond any doubt you were okay. But now it is evident not only to you but to everyone else, too. You are rejected. The why of it all doesn't matter anymore. It only matters that it happened ... and it hurts.

You feel fearful of the other relationships in your life. Will they reject you, too? Will you always feel as if you have "reject" stamped on your forehead?

Some days you begin to feel okay, then something happens and the old fear comes back. "I am going to be pushed away. I will never be secure again."

At times like these, you have a Savior whose arms are open wide to receive you, He listens with a tender acceptance you will find no where else.

O God, rejection hurts so deeply...

It comes suddenly and deliberately...
Without warning ... without a clue.
Its aim is specific. It makes its mark.

I go down aching in agony...
Triggered by emotions pushed down to silence.

The way back is slow ... but sure.
A new day dawns. I will tell Jesus.
I can see through my tears ... God is here.

Father, You tell me that You are close to the broken-hearted and that You save those who are crushed in spirit. My heart is broken ... my spirit is crushed.

Thank you for caring that I hurt. Thank you that Your unfailing love is my comfort ... thank you that I can say, "Praise be to the God and Father of our Lord Jesus Christ, the Father of compassion and the God of all comfort" ... thank you that You comfort me in all my troubles, so that I can comfort those in any trouble with the comfort I myself have received from You.

My heart aches. Help me to hold my head up . . . to keep on committing my pain to You. Then I will know the joy of a closer walk with You when other joys have failed. I will have Your perfect peace, for I have determined that my thoughts will stay on You.

"My comfort in my suffering is this: Your promise preserves my life."

(Psalm 119:50)

"The Lord is close to the brokenhearted and saves those who are crushed in spirit."

(Psalm 34:18)

REFLECTIONS

_____

_____

_____

_____

_____

_____

_____

_____

_____

DESPAIR

You know that no one likes to be around you when you are gloomy. In fact, you don't even like to be around yourself. You feel as if everyone can see the black cloud that hangs around your head like a halo. You also know that no one could possibly mistake it for a halo ... not on you.

Despair, gloom, hopelessness seem to be your companions right now. You didn't ask them to join you, but here they are ... unwelcomed, but very present intruders in your life. Things were going well. You seemed able to cope with some of the frustrations of being strong when "the other" was weak ... but then things took a turn for the worse and you lost it. The old questions come flooding back...

"Will I ever be different?"

"Will I ever be free?"

"Will I ever be a strong person, no matter what happens?"

And, with the questions come the despair, the gloominess, the hopelessness.

Dear one, God knows your heart and He longs for you to pour out your pain to Him. The difference, the freedom, the strength will come from Him.

Lord, I don't want to go on. My life is turning inside out ... I no longer know what is real. Who am I? Who are my friends? Who really loves me? Does anyone care? Does my life really matter? Why can't I just accept myself and enjoy what I'm doing ... the way others seem to. Why do I feel like such a failure? Why do I have this confusion in my mind? Why ... why ... why?

In all my anxiety ... in all my pain ... in all my heartbreak, I have one anchor to hold me—You are with me.

When I pray to You in agony...
    You listen.
When I cry out to You for hope...
    You hear my cries.

When I long for comfort in my hurting...
You are my comforter.

Thank you, dear Father, for caring about the things I care about... thank you that I matter to You... thank you for loving me enough to listen... to answer... and to encourage ... thank you for always being there and for being the anchor in my storms.

"... the Lord has heard my weeping. The Lord has heard my cry for mercy; the Lord accepts my prayer."

(Psalm 6:8–9)

"Trust in the Lord with all your heart and lean not on your own understanding. In all your ways acknowledge him, and he will make your paths straight."

(Proverbs 3:5–6)

REFLECTIONS

SHAME

Does everybody know? It feels as if everyone you meet has eyes to see into your very soul. You feel trapped by what you have done and eternally identified with your past behavior.

You know you have changed and will keep on changing, but in your heart of hearts you wonder if others will ever see you as anyone but a weak, groveling, embarrassing dolt. Surely that is what you became when you gave in against your will and violated your character. You feel that way. And probably they do, too. They really have no reason to think otherwise.

It's chilling to think what "the other" might have told them . . . but when you consider your behavior, your compromised integrity, then whatever was said was deserved. There is no doubt in your mind about that, but still it hurts.

You wonder where forgiveness comes in all of this. Do people ever forgive and go on?

You can be sure that God does . . . and right now you need to spend some time with Him. Stay with Him, unburdening your soul, until you can walk away . . . free at last.

Dear God . . . I am so ashamed of the person I have become. I search my heart, wondering why it happened . . . when. How could I have been so blind? I feel so foolish . . . what must others think of me?

I am ashamed. . .

   . . . of the exclusivity of my relationship.
   . . . of being controlled . . . and controlling.
   . . . of depending on another to give my life value and
      inspiration. . .
   . . . of being too important in someone else's life, their
      savior.

I have been wrong in many, many ways . . . I am so sorry. I ask You to forgive me and to "Search me, O God, and know my heart; test me and know my anxious thoughts. See if there is any offensive way in me, and lead me in the way everlasting (Psalm 139:23–24).

I am grateful to you for revealing to me those things in my life which are grievous to you, and still not holding them against me . . . thank you that "there is no condemnation in Christ Jesus" (Romans 8:1).

Thank you for loving me enough to convict me of the wrongs in my relationships . . . for not allowing me to rest in those wrongs. I feel humiliated . . . embarrassed . . . even angry. I know I have failed . . . but I will change. By Your grace, I will change.

"May my heart be blameless toward your decrees, that I may not be put to shame."

(Psalm 119:80)

"Do your best to present yourself to God as one approved, a workman who does not need to be ashamed and who correctly handles the word of truth."

(2 Timothy 2:15)

REFLECTIONS

_____

_____

_____

_____

_____

_____

_____

DISTRACTIONS

You find it so hard to concentrate. You read and your mind wanders. You think and you find your mind becomes a wide screen where memories roll by like a bad movie.

You hate it, but it seems so difficult to block out thoughts. They come in all shapes and sizes. There are thoughts of anger, thoughts of tender times, thoughts of arguments, thoughts of intimacies shared, thoughts of places visited . . . overwhelming thoughts of the bitter and the sweet that make up memories of life with the one to whom you were so close.

Sometimes the pain prevails. Sometimes the joy is primary. No matter which one, your thoughts are not your own, under your control. They wander aimlessly and land where they will.

The restlessness in your mind lets you know there's something wrong.

There is only One to whom you can go for peace . . . He is the Prince of Peace who waits for you.

Father, please forgive me. I now see what You have tried to show me . . . I see why I have not had the peace I longed for. I have said "no" to the way You have told me to think. I have held on to hurting memories which continue to cause pain. My mind drifts to the "what if's" . . . to words spoken in anger. I have failed to determine to forget what is behind and reach for what lies ahead, pressing on toward the goal. I have chosen, instead, to allow the past to come into the present . . . to grieve over what has been . . . to long for what cannot be. I have chosen to disobey You.

Help me, Father, to begin again! I want to saturate my mind with Your Word. I must refuse to think on things which pull me down except to learn from them . . . then I must let them go. Help me, Father, to do this. Worry . . . fear . . . anguish . . . painful thinking is a way of life with me. I know I cannot change unless You change me. But, I am willing. I want to please You.

"You will guard him and keep him in perfect and constant peace whose mind (both its inclination and its character) is stayed on You, because he commits himself to You, leans on You and hopes confidently in you."

(Isaiah 26:3, Amplified)

"Cast all your anxiety on him because he cares for you."
(1 Peter 5:7)

REFLECTIONS

WALLS

You have done a good job. Brick by brick, you have built an impenetrable barrier that protects you from the feelings that have been so painful for so long. Over and over you have told yourself that you don't care anymore. You have convinced yourself that numbness is a preferred state.

The wall keeps people at a distance where they are manageable. It provides a security that you believe you need and deserve. At first it seemed lonely, but now you have adapted and the barrier has become a friend. Sometimes you long for someone to cross the wall ... but then you remember the hurts ... the disappointments. And, the fantasy you entertain that you could be free and open with someone else disappears and, once again, you remember that you are surrounded by a wall of your own making.

Your Father knows about your self-protection. He longs to have you turn to Him for the only true protection there is.

Father, I feel shattered ... and so alone. The wall within me is tall ... strong ... and cold. I smile from my position of safety behind it. I appear to be friendly and warm. I say what I believe others want to hear ... anything to keep them from noticing the wall. Almost nothing can touch me, though someone's caring and understanding sometimes causes the wall to weaken. I must be cautious and quick to guard it. I am alone behind my wall ... alone with memories that are bitter reminders of pain and brokenness.

O God, I know that walls do not bring unity. They speak of hurts ... of distance ... of bondage to the past ... of unforgiveness. They do not bring about the oneness that Jesus prayed His people would have with each other (John 17). They do not encourage reconciliation among believers. They do not allow us to bear each others' burdens (Galatians 6:2) that we might encourage one another (1 Thessalonians 5:13).

I know that I must allow my walls to come down ... for other people to know me and accept me just as I am. They must come down for me to reach out in love ... for me to be accepting and forgiving, regardless of anything else. If I am willing to be open ... and honest ... and vulnerable, ... perhaps You could even use me in the life of someone else ... and them in my life ... that together we could grow to be the people You created us to be. I am willing, dear Father, for You to work this out in me.

"May they be brought to complete unity to let the world know that you sent me and have loved them even as you have loved me."

(John 17:23)

"One thing I do: Forgetting what is behind and straining toward what is ahead, I press on toward the goal to win the prize for which God has called me heavenward in Christ Jesus."

(Philippians 3:13–14)

REFLECTIONS

LOSS OF IDENTITY

You wonder how you could have been swallowed up in the life, the personality, the ambitions, the identity of "the other." How could it have happened?

At first you just wanted to help. You saw someone who seemed to need another to come alongside, to pick up the other side of the log. But then it was as if you couldn't tell who was carrying what. Were you helping with the log? Were you being helped? Did you lend a hand? Did you need a hand? The "you" that you believed you knew slowly became absorbed in "the other" and you became a different person. You were the last to recognize the loss of your identity. Others had seen it. Some had bravely told you that you were different, that you were a changed person. You tried to ignore the incredulous look in their eyes and tried to pretend you were hearing compliments. But deep inside you knew that your identity had been swallowed.

Now you know it. You recognize the loss, but surely it is not permanent? How can "you" disappear?

God knows exactly where you are, but better than that, He knows who you are. Your identity is safe with Him. Take your confusion to Him. He is waiting to heal your hurting mind.

Father ... I don't know what to think. I believed that by this time in my life I would have everything together ... I would have reached my goals ... I would know how I feel, what I think, who I am. Instead, I feel lost and empty, as though I exist in a mist ... drifting. The closest person in the world to me has gone ... we are no longer a part of each others' lives. My security ... my value ... my sense of who I am rested in our relationship. And now it's gone.

Father, I know that I must find another way. I must not settle for anything but Your truths ... I must not place my significance in my alliance with another person. My identity must be in who I am in You. ...

You chose me. I have been adopted by You ... I am Your child, born again into Your family. You know my name and I am precious to You. I am new in You. I am not condemned ... my sins are forgiven. I have a new heart ... and Your Spirit. I have Your strength to keep on going ... even in the very midst of this heaviness, this darkness. I can come boldly to You for mercy and find grace to help in my need. You are conforming me to the image of Christ and You have given me all that I need for life and godliness. You love me very much ... with an everlasting love ... and nothing in the world can ever separate me from Your great love for me.

"Your Spirit himself bears witness with my spirit that I am your child, and if your child, then heir–your heir and joint heir with Christ, if indeed I suffer with Him, that we may also be glorified together."

(Romans 8:16–17 paraphrased)

Please help me remember...

REFLECTIONS

THE NEED TO PLEASE OTHERS

Sometimes you lose yourself in your scramble to please others. It's not that you mind the normal giving that God calls you to as a believer. But, the problem comes when you begin to explain every little action. You feel as if everyone expects you to live up to *their* standard and if you fail, then maybe you can make them understand why you did what you did.

Your friends say you are defensive. That cuts to the quick every time you hear it because that is not a Christ-like quality. The Scriptures say He didn't try to explain Himself even though He was right and His accusers were wrong.

But, where is the fine line between "letting things gO' and explaining yourself so people around you will understand and love you better because you are right?

That's really the bottom line. If you aren't understood, then they won't love you . . . or is it, if you aren't loved, you won't be understood?

When the struggle rages, make some time to turn to Him. He understands.

Father, I am weary of struggling.

Why do I feel that I must earn love? I must work hard enough and long enough. I must be good enough . . . I must succeed. I must say the right things at the right time and with the right expression. I must feel right, act right and look right. I must not fail . . . for if I do, I will feel unlovable . . . unaccept-able. I will be rejected . . . and the rejection will kill me.

Lord, I'm so very tired of these games . . . tired of masks . . . tired of trying . . . tired of living the impossible lie.

Let me rest in Your love . . . Your love which is everlasting and unconditional . . . Your love which is patient and kind . . . which is not easily angered . . . which keeps no record of my wrongs. Your love guides me, protects me, and gives me hope. It never fails. You love me . . . just because You want to love me.

O Father, let me be comforted by Your promises. . .
comforted by Truth from Your Word. . .
comforted by Your Word with its hope. . .
comforted by Your hope in my heart. . .
comforted in my heart by Your love.

Teach me to be me as I grow to be like You. Remind me that to please You is enough . . . and that I don't have to struggle.

"Who shall separate us from the love of Christ? Shall trouble or hardship or persecution or famine or nakedness or danger or sword? . . .. For I am convinced that neither death nor life, neither angels nor demons, neither the present nor the future, nor any powers, neither height nor depth, nor anything else in all creation, will be able to separate us from the love of God that is in Christ Jesus our Lord."

(Romans 8:35, 38)

REFLECTIONS

THE NEED FOR PARENTAL APPROVAL

You know your need for parental approval is affecting your other relationships. Those close to you in your adulthood are disbelieving at how a call from home ... or the absence of a call from home ... can cause you to slip into such a slump.

For months you do fine, and then the holidays come. Your mother decides to write or come for a visit. That's when you become a little child again, waiting for a word of approval. You do things you'd rather not do just because she says you must. You allow your need for approval to dominate your behavior. But family and friends are appalled at your gutless acquiescence. They are no more appalled than you. You feel so powerless, so small, so child-like.

You chew on your fingernail as you wrestle with the dismayed response of those who love you now and the disapproving response of a parent whose love you have always wanted.

There is only one thing to do when you find yourself confronted with the conflict in your soul ... take it all to your heavenly Father and talk it over with Him. He approves of you just because you are His child.

O Father, what is wrong with me? I struggle. I am compelled to achieve ... to win. I feel I must be what I am afraid I cannot be. How I long to be able to just enjoy life.

But, it will have to be later ... it's always later ... the leisurely and lasting things must wait. Today I must try again to be all my mother has always wanted me to be. I hope I will do the right thing. I must not disappoint her.

I realize I may never be able to be who my mother wants me to be. I love her and I honor her. I can be kind and caring, but I cannot always meet her demands and wishes. Help me to overcome my weakness of allowing her to dominate me. Help me, Father, to focus on pleasing You.

You say it pleases You for me to belong to You (Ephesians 1:4–5) . . . that You are conforming my character to the character of Jesus Christ (Romans 8:29) . . . and that You have given me all I need to become the person You created me to be. I want to please You by continually abiding in You . . . by depending only upon You.

Thank you for all You are doing in my life. Thank you for accepting me. Thank you for loving me . . . just because You want to love me.

"His divine power has given us everything we need for life and godliness through our knowledge of him who called us by his own glory and goodness."

(2 Peter 1:3)

"How great is your goodness, which you have stored up for those who fear you, which you bestow in the sight of men on those who take refuge in you. In the shelter of your presence you hide them from the intrigues of men; in your dwelling you keep them safe from accusing tongues."

(Psalm 31:19–20)

REFLECTIONS

_____

_____

_____

_____

_____

_____

_____

DEPENDENCY

It is hard to believe that you have actually lost. The battle is over. The steps toward independence have been painfully followed and now, you're there. You have discovered your ability to control your own thoughts, to be responsible for your own emotions, but now that you are free, you are also sad.

To leave anything that is familiar, even when it has been painful, gives you a feeling of loss, of grief. And, that is where you are just now. In one moment, you are teetering on the brink of moving on to a fuller, more satisfying life. In the next moment, you want to cry.

God knows his child. He knows your pain. He knows how it has felt for you to assume a healthy independence ... and He cares. Tell Him how you feel.

O God ... the one I love has gone from me ... the one I trusted like no one else in the world ... the one to whom I turned in good times and bad ... the one on whom I leaned ... the one who brought me such security ... such joy ... who made me feel like somebody. My heart groans within me. What will I do? How can I go on?

In an instant, Your Spirit within me whispers...

"Trust in the Lord with all your heart and lean not on your own understanding. . . ."

(Proverbs 3:5)

"It is better to take refuge in the Lord than to trust in man."

(Psalm 118:8)

"Trust in him at all times, O people; pour out your hearts to him, for God is our refuge."

(Psalm 62:8)

"Those who know your name will trust in you, for you, Lord, have never forsaken those who seek you."

(Psalm 9:10)

Father, I know that You are worthy of my trust ... of my devotion ... of my faithfulness. I choose to depend upon You rather than upon anyone else ... to care about me ... to listen to me ... to protect me ... to give me value ... to give my life meaning ... to love me. O God, help me to cling to You and no one else ... and to trust You with all my heart.

REFLECTIONS

DISAPPOINTMENT

There is no way you can get around the fact that your disappointment has its roots in what you expected. The very word itself smacks of "missed appointments" with love, with acceptance, with freedom, with fulfillment.

Your expectations were based on what you thought you could legitimately expect. The shock has been that you thought wrong. The question keeps coming up, "What if we had met when my thinking was right?" or "What if we had fewer expectations of one another?"

This is where you can begin to trust the sovereignty of God. That doesn't make the pain go away, but it surely reminds you that everything is not in your control. Once you learn that God is greater than your timing or your thinking, you can let go of your disappointment and begin to look for His divine appointments.

Be honest with Him when you lay your heart before Him.

My hopes have faded . . . my dreams are dashed. . . I feel so let down . . . I have such a sense of sorrow for the way things turned out.

O God, I am almost overwhelmed with disappointment as I look back on a relationship which had been so fulfilling. What happened to the fun times, the encouragement, the sharing of our hearts? What happened to the challenges to go higher . . . the confidences we entrusted . . . the counsel in times of wondering . . . the comfort of just being in each others' company?

But, Father, I know that, once again, I have a choice to make. I can sit here and reminisce . . . and regret . . . and wish . . . and weep . . . or I can face the reality of a relationship which drifted into the domination of dependency. I can acknowledge my responsibility for not responding the way I knew was right. I can confess my disobedience to You. I can accept the fact that we cannot continue this way and be in Your will.

Thank you that You are the Lord who redeems my mistakes ... Thank you that You are the Lord of beginning again ... Thank you that You are the Lord of another chance. Thank you that You are the Lord who loves me ... just because You want to love me. Thank you for Your Word which says...

"Weeping may remain for a night, but rejoicing comes in the morning."

(Psalm 30:5)

"I will bless the Lord who has counseled me; Indeed, my mind instructs me in the night. I have set the Lord continually before me; Because He is at my right hand, I will not be shaken."

(Psalm 16:7−9)

Thank you that I do not have to go on living with these haunting feelings of disappointment. I can listen to You and learn how a relationship which could have been so precious grew into habitual misery when left unguarded by Your truths. I can walk closer to You and allow You to rule in my every area of my life.

REFLECTIONS

_____

_____

_____

_____

_____

_____

DISCOURAGEMENT

Discouragement can feel like a cold, wet wool blanket clinging to your bare, wet skin on a hot day. It's uncomfortable. It's irritating. You want to get rid of it, but it adheres to you . . . wet on wet, until you deliberately tear it away.

For you, discouragement has come as a surprise. You have made your plans for new behavior. You have determined that you will no longer be affected by the actions of "the other," the one you have let control your feelings for so long. You have taken steps to pursue new thoughts, new relationships, new activities, and now, without warning, the memories have come rushing in.

This time it isn't the usual sickening reminder of the arguments, the anger or the agony of continual conflict. This time it's a bittersweet remembrance of good times. Suddenly, out of no where, or was it really out of somewhere, you hear a song, you smell a fragrance, you pass a certain street, and there it is . . . a memory of a moment that can never be recaptured. But your heart is pulled. Your mind is drawn back to vain toying with "What if. . . ?" and "If only. . . ." and "Was I mistaken?"

With a sickening rush of reality, the truth surges in. Life has moved on. You have changed. The relationship has been irretrievably altered. And you realize that today is today and that there is no yesterday to call home to. Discouragement settles in to cling to you . . . to bring sadness to your soul. You thought you had moved beyond these emotions. That seems to hurt the most.

But, there is hope. You will get better. It will take time. Take some time to turn to Jesus. . .

O Lord, I am so discouraged . . . by people whom I love . . . by shattered dreams . . . by all the failures . . . I don't think I can go on. . .

And yet, You remind me that even when I struggle. . .

I am to endure as a good soldier of Christ Jesus. . . and You say. . .
I can do all things because You will strengthen me. . .

I can thank you for this time ... You will cause it to work for my good...
You are for me ... You accept me... always...
I can safely trust You and obey You ... because You love me...

Lord, these memories are painful to me and they are so discouraging. In my own strength, I cannot battle the emotions that overwhelm me. I ask You to remind me that, through Your strength, I can control my thoughts. I want to be free of discouragement...free to be the person You created me to be. I pray that You will remind me that I am to bring each thought to You ... and to leave it with You. I know that it is a choice that I must continually make as these hurts heal. Because of You, I can ... I will ... go on.

"Endure hardship ... like a good soldier of Christ Jesus."
(2 Timothy 2:3)

"I can do everything through him who gives me strength."
(Philippians 4:13)

REFLECTIONS

_____

_____

_____

_____

_____

_____

_____

GUILT

Anger flashes in your eyes long after you choose to forgive the one who hurt you. The memory of the painful relationship is like a nightmare . . . invasive . . . horrifying. Why does it cause such anger if you have really forgiven? Could it be you need to turn the forgiveness toward yourself? Could it be the anger is a reminder of the disgust and embarrassment you feel over what you have done . . . over how you have acted? Could it be? Forgiveness, giving up the right to punish, applies to you as well as to others. You are as needy of that release from yourself as are your enemies.

If you cannot release yourself, if you cannot let go of the guilt and the shame, then one day you will find that you are bitter. Deep roots of unforgiveness will have taken hold and you will find a sadness in your eyes you never expected to be there . . . and it hurts. To forgive yourself brings you to the point where you are willing to accept what Christ has already freely done for you.

If this is difficult for you, go to the Lord and let Him carry the guilt that He has already taken care of.

O God . . . I know that I am to forgive others, and I do . . . my love for them is great. It's me, dear Lord, it's the very thought of me that stirs my anger . . . that makes me ashamed . . . that keeps me awake . . . that eats away at me.

How could I have been so blind . . . so insensitive? How could I have compromised? Why didn't I stand? Why didn't I see? What was I thinking . . . and what must others think of me?

I sometimes feel almost overwhelmed, living with these regrets . . . remembering how weak I am . . . weeping over the pain that I have caused.

Yet, in my heart I know that I cannot continue to mourn and to punish myself for that which I cannot change. I cannot allow these feelings to rob me of Your peace and joy any longer. I must allow You to teach me through my mistakes . . . I must allow Your Word to heal my hurts.

*And, Father, I know that Your way is forgiveness . . .
that You do not condemn me. Surely I cannot think so highly of
myself as to refuse to let go of that which You have forgiven.*

*So, in obedience to You, I willingly forgive myself for
what I have done . . . for the person I have been. I do not excuse
it, but I seek Your wisdom to learn from it. I am determined to
live in victory by allowing You to control what I think and
what I do . . . that I may become the person You created me to
be.*

" Forgetting what is behind and straining toward what is
ahead, I press on toward the goal to win the prize for which God
has called me heavenward in Christ Jesus."

(Philippians 3:13–14)

"Do not call to mind the former things, or ponder things of
the past."

(Isaiah 43:18 NASB)

REFLECTIONS

INFERIORITY

Feeling inferior is not something you like to talk about. You don't exactly feel comfortable calling an acquaintance and saying, "I feel so inferior tonight." But, in reality, that is exactly how you feel . . . damaged, not up to par, unacceptable, not good enough.

If you told anyone, they would probably say, "Oh, don't be silly. You have it all together! You are bright, successful . . . how could you feel inferior?" The encouragement is kind but not very helpful. Somehow you can't believe what other well-intentioned acquaintances tell you.

You know who you are. You know what you are. You know what you've done. And, you know how it feels to be a dingy, yellow, T-shirt next to everyone else's white tuxedo.

So, you just don't talk about it. Who wants constantly to be prodded to believe something that mocks the way you think.

You can turn to the One who is always there to listen. He will never call you silly. He understands how you feel and values you as precious.

Lord, there are times I feel so unimportant . . . so alone . . . as though I don't belong anywhere . . . I am nobody . . .

Then . . . in sweetness . . . in quietness . . . Your Spirit speaks to my heart and gently reminds me . . .

You are always with me . . . wherever I go . . .
  even when I don't feel Your presence . . .
  I belong to You . . . I am part of Your family . . .
    You call me by name . . . I am the apple of Your eye . . .
  You have carved me on the palm of Your hands . . .
  You have a purpose for my life . . .

Father, teach me to walk in light of these Truths . . . to focus my thoughts on You . . . and who I am because of You . . .

not on how I feel. It won't be easy for me ... You didn't say it would be. But, I can chose ... for I am Yours.

"In my anguish I cried to the Lord, and he answered by setting me free. The Lord is with me...."

(Psalm 118:5-6)

"Be content with what you have, because God has said, 'Never will I leave you; never will I forsake you.'"

(Hebrews 13:5)

REFLECTIONS

_____

_____

_____

_____

_____

_____

_____

_____

_____

_____

_____

_____

JEALOUSY

It's hard to believe that you are jealous. You have always hated to see jealous people live out their petty paranoia. It always made them look so foolish...

Now the one that looks foolish is you.

You have tried to keep a cap on it. You've tried to hide your feelings. You've tried to hold your tongue, but somehow catty, cutting words slip past your tightly clinched teeth every time you think of what "the other," the one you have loved, the one you have always trusted, is doing. Every time you think of losing, the ache inside becomes unbearable and it releases the poisonous acid of jealous rage.

Jealousy is eating away at you and you hate it. It has become like a monster lurking behind your heart, and just when you think you have driven the devilish emotion out, there it is in all of its indelicate, obnoxious glory.

In your heart of hearts you wonder if there is hope for pain like this. The situation isn't going to change. The one you love seems to care less, even denying you have anything to be concerned about.

The questions keep on coming. Will it always be this way? Will I always feel this hatred and fear of losing?

Sadly, the answer is "yes" until you are ready to call the vicious emotion by its awful, ugly name—jealousy. Then with your broken heart in your hand, turn to Jesus, the mender of broken hearts.

Dear Lord, what is jealousy? Some say it's a sign of love ... of caring. Some think it's exciting ... evidence of connected souls. But, I have known the resentment ... the fear ... the selfishness ... the possessiveness ... the control ... the dependency.

Jealousy ... I know it as the tortured, self-centered cry of a heart in agony over the threat of loss. Jealousy shows a lack of trust in You ... and that is wrong.

O Father, teach me freedom in trusting You with all that touches me. Remind me that to love another is not to possess, but to seek the best ... and the best is not what pleases me, but what pleases You. Help me to remember that I must hold all my relationships in an open hand ... that You might be able to work within our lives as they intertwine.

"For jealousy enrages a man. ..."

(Proverbs 7:34)

"Jealousy is as severe as Sheol; Its flashes are flashes of fire. ..."

(Song of Solomon 8:6)

I do not want to be enraged ... or reflect flashes of fire. I want to trust You totally and completely, knowing that You, in love, will freely give me all that is good for me.

Teach me that losing is not the end. Remind me that You are always there ... no matter who comes and goes in my life. Give me the faith to believe You. ..

REFLECTIONS

POSSESSIVENESS

You feel caged.

You wanted to provide a place of belonging, instead you found yourself possessed. The one you longed to care for became your possessor.

How could it happen? The beginning was so good . . . it all seemed so right . . . but then you began to feel trapped in a situation of your own making. But your motives were good, weren't they? You want to have a pure heart.

You battle in your mind with the rightness of protecting yourself versus providing the care that seems to be needed. You struggle with the boundaries. You draw a line that seems reasonable, and the war begins. Part of you that you believed you had reclaimed is up for grabs once again. You struggle with feelings of loss for giving in and feelings of guilt for holding on.

You wonder why you still wrestle with this when you thought you were doing so well.

Give yourself time to sort it out as you take it to the One who knows the innermost longing of your soul.

O Father, You know my heart is to help others. I want to reach out and lend a hand . . . to encourage . . . to be a friend. I want to be there when I am needed . . . I want to comfort . . . and support. But, there are times I feel clutched at . . . smothered . . . like a prisoner . . . controlled.

It's the phone calls throughout the day and night. It's the unexpected drop-ins. It's always wanting me to be there to listen . . . to understand . . . to do something. It's the questions . . . the expectations . . . the demands . . .the manipulation . . . the gifts. It's the lack of freedom. It's the frustrations.

I fight feelings of resentment.

Lord, teach me to lovingly set limits on my time with those who tend to hold on to me. Teach me the appropriate boundaries that I might teach the one who is suffocating me . . .

trying to stay too close. Show me how to help, to encourage, to be supportive, to be a friend within the delicate framework of the lines I must draw.

Father, I know that our dependency ... our trust ... must be in You ... not in others. You are the one who fulfills our needs ... who never fails ... who is always faithful ... who is always there ... who always cares. Teach each of us to cling only to You ...

"And my God will meet all your needs according to his glorious riches in Christ Jesus."

(Philippians 4:19)

"Do not be anxious about anything, but in everything, by prayer and petition, with thanksgiving, present your requests to God."

(Philippians 4:6)

REFLECTIONS

_____

_____

_____

_____

_____

_____

_____

_____

_____

REGRET

In your heart of hearts there is a door, closed but not sealed, that blocks the entrance to a room filled with regrets. When you enter that door, the painful sensations overtake you as "what might have been" clings to you like an invisible web.

You go there less and less as time separates you and "the other." You make a sincere effort to avoid even going near the door because you know in your conscious mind how futile it is. But in your sleep, there are times your dreams become visitations to the Room of Regret. You wake up feeling drained, bothered, wistful, and then you remember where you have spent the night . . . in a place where you have no control . . . in a place where things can never change . . . and it leaves you hurting . . . depressed . . . defeated.

You know that you can't go back. This is one of those "make the most of it" situations, always easier to say than do.

You can turn to the One who promises to cause all things, even your regrets, to work for good. You can still learn, and grow, and change. God will give you room . . . when others say "It will never happen." Take some time to spend with Him. He loves you.

O God . . . it's the regrets . . . the painful, nagging, haunting regrets. I agonize over them . . . the broken promises . . . chilling words . . . crushing accusations . . . cold manipulations . . . the walls of silence. Regrets tear at my heart. If only I had seen what was happening . . . if only I had responded differently . . . if only I had behaved honestly and lovingly . . . if only. . . .

But, Father, I know it's time to go on. It's time to get up from where I've fallen . . . time to begin again. It's time to quit pondering those things which I can no longer change. Forgive me for what I have done to You and to others I love.

Help me, I pray, from this time on to live in love. . . .

To be patient and kind. . .

Not to envy ... not to boast ... not to be proud...
Not to be self-seeking ... not easily angered...
To keep no record of wrongs...
Not to delight in evil..
To rejoice with the truth...
To always protect ... always trust...
always hope ... always persevere.

Help me, Father, never to allow my love to fail... but to be a reflection of Jesus ... to love as He loves. Teach me to so love in all my ways that I will not have to regret how I have behaved toward You or toward anyone touched by my life.

"So then whatever you desire that others would do to and for you, even so do you also to and for them, for this sums up the Law and the prophets."

(Matthew 7:12, Amplified)

REFLECTIONS

_____

_____

_____

_____

_____

_____

_____

_____

FEAR OF THE FUTURE

"I will always be part of your life." Those words seem to be such a lie now. The promise seemed so secure. "The other" seemed so sincere. Now the promise is broken and "the other" is gone. You are left to face the future with a different set of challenges than you ever thought you would have.

You can look back now and see how you put too much stock in what another person could provide in your life. You look back now and see the truth of the statement, "Futures have a way of falling down in mid-flight." And you can vouch for the fact they can fall with very little warning.

But now, here you are. You are alive. You are well and it looks as if God may grant you a long life. It just seems like that might be the way it is. There is a whole big future out there. And if the truth were really known, you are frightened and full of fear. You know where you need to turn. You've gone to Him over and over, but this fear seems almost too big ... even for God.

Why not take the risk that the One who is the same yesterday, today, and tomorrow might have an answer for you?

O God ... just when I thought my life was settled ... just when I felt comfortable and secure ... just when I believed we would grow old gracefully ... together ... my world has been turned upside down. Instead of feeling safe, settled and secure, I battle feelings of panic and pessimism. I am afraid of what the future holds.

I am afraid of ...
... having no one with whom I can share my life ...
... the doubts and disappointments
... the cares and confidences
... not really being liked now that I'm "single"
... feeling empty ...
... this void inside me never going away ...

But, Father, I know my fears are not according to Your truths. I know that, as I focus on You, my fears will fade and my faith will grow.

I love Your Word which says...

"For I am the Lord, your God, who takes hold of your right hand and says to you, 'Do not fear; I will help you.'"

(Isaiah 41:13)

Thank you that I don't have to be afraid ... thank you for who You are ... thank you that I can safely trust in You because You...
... know all things (Psalm 139:2–4).
... have all power (Jeremiah 32:17).
... are present everywhere (Jeremiah 23:23–24).
... are patient (Psalm 86:15).
... are faithful (Hebrews 10:23).
... are merciful (Psalm 103:8).
... rule over all (1 Chronicles 29:11–13).

Thank you that I don't have to be afraid because I know I can always depend on You. I know that You love me ... just because You want to love me.

REFLECTIONS

LOSS OF FRIENDSHIPS

You always wanted the security of a best friend ... You never really felt attached to anyone ... even to family ... because they *had* "to take you in."

Deep in your heart, you want to have a friend who will always be there, no matter what. Deep in your heart you believe you *need* a friend who will be there for you always.

But somehow, just when you thought you had found such a friend, the whole situation began to sour. At first it was little disagreements, small irritations that hurt deeper than they should have. They hurt so much because the relationship meant everything. The good was so good, that it seemed unbelievable that the small things could be so bad.

Now the friendship is irrevocably changed. It will never be the same. And, in reality, you wouldn't want it to be the same, but today you miss your friend. You miss the good times. You wonder if you will ever have anyone besides family who will always be there.

Why does something so precious have to be accompanied by such pain?

You wonder if your friend ever has the difficult memories that you do. You know you shouldn't ask, but it surely would be a comfort to know that someone else is struggling, too. Isn't that what friends are for?

Then you remember. There is One who sticks closer than a brother... why not take the time to turn to Him?

Father, I ask You to teach me how to love my friends ... how to give them the right place in my life ... how to place them in the right perspective, according to Your will. My tendency, O Father, is to choose one ... one I love and who loves me ... one to talk with ... one to laugh with ... one to share with ... one to care for ... one to care for me. How easily I come to depend upon that one ... to want that one to depend upon me. How easily You fade into the background ... how easily my friend takes Your place in my life.

Help me to cultivate new relationships ... to develop new interests ... to give my love and attention to You first and foremost ... and after that, to friends. Give me the heart to love without first being loved, to serve without needing praise, to give without expecting anything in return.

Help me, I pray, to focus on You ... to give You supremacy, first place, in every thought that I have, in each word that I say, in all that I do.

Help me to remember Your words to ...

"Love the Lord your God with all your heart and with all your soul and with all your mind."

(Matthew 22:37)

Help me to remember that this is the first and greatest commandment ... help me to love You first and then to love my friends.

REFLECTIONS

PAINFUL MEMORIES

It haunts you each time you see the little verse, "God gave us memories that we might have roses in December."

Your memories are a bouquet of roses and weeds, daisies and thorns . . . all mixed together. December's special days bring a melancholy fragrance, aromatic and memorable . . . but never again the sweet, pure smell of roses. You know God promises that everything that comes along will work together for good . . . will be blended into the aromas of life. But you miss the pure, sweet smell of roses. You miss the memories that are pleasant. More than that, you miss the substance of the relationship. You miss the good days with "the other."

In this world, there are no guarantees that another will always be there. You are realistic. You know that. You just never thought that the guarantees would break down with this relationship. But they did . . . and still life goes on.

Your Heavenly Father knows your painful memories. He was there when they were made, so He will understand when you pour out your heart to Him.

Father, these memories . . . memories of special days . . . smother my mind and kindle a melancholy mood within me. The nostalgia of warm and wonderful celebrations together is sweet and sad. We never dreamed they would end . . . we somehow assumed we would grow old together. Now those times are over. Another birthday . . . another Christmas . . . another holiday . . . another vacation. Sometimes a phone call and sometimes not. Nothing is the same.

Remembering is bittersweet. In the beginning there was laughter . . . care-free hours of enjoyment . . . surprises . . . hours of sharing the deep and meaningful reflections of our hearts. As time went on, what we expected from one another grew . . . the ties that bind became chains that enslaved. We were suffocated by the exclusivity of our relationship. And, now it's over.

O Father, sometimes I ache . . . sometimes I don't feel at all. I know I must forgive the broken promises . . . the disappointments. I will remember to be thankful for the good times . . . the lessons learned. I acknowledge the good intentions and confess the wrongness of this relationship. I accept my responsibility in its failure. Now I will focus on becoming who You want me to be, on aiding in You, on living according to Your will.

"Now therefore I pray You, if I have found favor in Your sight, show me now Your way, that I may know You (progressively become more deeply and intimately acquainted with You, perceiving and recognizing and understanding more strongly and clearly) that I may find favor in Your sight" (Exodus 33:13, Amplified Bible).

And, now, what does the Lord my God require of me, but to fear Him, to walk in all His ways and to love Him, to serve Him with all my heart and with all my soul? (Deuteronomy 10:12 paraphrased).

REFLECTIONS

_____

_____

_____

_____

_____

_____

_____

_____

LONELINESS

The hardest part of the day comes as the sun goes down. Twilight brings the rush for home, but home just isn't the same.

The quietness is deafening when you open the front door. The house is just the way you left it in the morning. Nothing can warm the chill that the silence brings.

You miss the sense of being attached even though there was so much pain. At least you felt something. At least there was sensation even if it did feel like a constant ache. Being attached fed the hunger of your soul to be united with something, someone, that would make you feel whole.

When you met you gave in to manipulation and guilt just to have someone there when you wanted two for dinner, when the tickets to the play came in twos, when the invitation was for a duo. You gave in and bent and changed who you were, what you believed, just for the company. Now, it's over and you ache with the loneliness.

You have a Father who understands. You have a Savior who has known loneliness ... and longs to hear from you.

O Father, the days drift by in wearisome repetition ... the nights scream in silence ... life seems cold, indifferent. A sense of sadness overwhelms me. Remembering is all that is left. I feel alone ...and lonely....

I know, dear Father, that You do not intend for me to go my own way ... by myself. Your heart is in relationships ... with You and with others who love You. You do not want me to be a loner ... or lonely.

O God, remind me of Your goodness to me ... of Your loving kindness so richly poured out ... of Your grace and graciousness ... of Your life given for me ... that I would be filled with Your Spirit ... that Your character would flow from me to others.

I will begin today to reach out...

I will cultivate new friendships by being friendly. . .
I will lend a hand to someone with a need. . .
I will encourage the fainthearted. . .
I will pray when I am alone . . . or lonely. . .
I will share Your love. . .

"Let your light shine before men, that they may see your good deeds and praise your Father in heaven."
(Matthew 5:16)

"Be kind and compassionate to one another, . . ."
(Ephesians 4:32)

REFLECTIONS

_____

_____

_____

_____

_____

_____

_____

_____

_____

_____

_____

_____

FEELINGS OF USELESSNESS

You feel if all this relationship turmoil had not happened, you could be useful. In your heart you question if God can use anyone who seemed to miss His will so badly?

You didn't mean to miss what was right in His sight, but because your thinking was so out of step with His, you did. You know now that there was no way He could have used you when you were trapped in that relationship, but now that you are no longer involved, you feel no longer useful.

God says your total dependence is to be on Him, and you often wonder, "Where is the balance?" He put a God-shaped vacuum within you to be filled by Him alone. But, there is also a deep need to be soul-connected with other humans. There is a longing to depend and to be depended upon ... but once that becomes bent, twisted, and perverted, the whole picture blurs.

You long to be useful. It's as simple as that. You can know that the Lord understands. My friend, pour out your feelings and know He sees you as a vessel in whom the treasure of His precious Son dwells. If you ever dare to see yourself through His eyes, your feelings of being useless will disappear. So take time and tell Him how you feel.

It wasn't so long ago, Father, that I felt vibrant and needed. I lived the good life the way I wanted to live it ... with whom I wanted to live it. Now that person is gone. My life has become dull and uninteresting as I go through the motions of living each day. I feel used ... unneeded ... unwanted ... useless.

And yet, Lord, there is something inside me which tells me I am not useless to You ... that I am valuable to You ... that I am needed. I search Your Word and plead before You to know what You would have me do. What are my responsibilities before You?

You show me that Your plan for me is to...

... share Your gospel (Mark 16:15)
... glorify You by my lifestyle (Matthew 5:13–16)
... serve others (Matthew 25:35–40)
... give to others (1 John 3:16–18)
... bear the burdens of other people (Galatians 6:2)
... pray (1 Thessalonians 4:17)
... follow the example of Jesus (1 Peter 2:21)
... be an example to the believers in speech, life, love, faith and purity (1 Thessalonians 4:12)

Forgive me, I pray, for forgetting that I belong to You ... that I am the temple of Your Spirit, whom I received as a gift from You. I am not my own ... I was bought for a price— purchased with a preciousness and paid for, made Your own. May I honor You and bring glory to You...

Thank you that You have plans for me, plans for welfare and not for calamity to give me a future and a hope.

REFLECTIONS

_____

_____

_____

_____

_____

_____

_____

_____

FEELING UNLOVED

Well, it happened again. You heard those mocking words that always seem to snicker as they fall from other people's lips. "I love you. I think you're one special person." It seems silly to find nice phrases like those offensive, but you always seem to doubt the sincerity of those comments.

What's there to love about you? What's so special about you? Somehow, you just can't see anything loveable. You are kind . . . some of the time . . . but many times you are just plain difficult and who wants to put up with that?

"If I'm so loveable, why aren't I loved by the people who mean the most to me?"

"If they ever got to know me, they wouldn't think so much of me."

On and on the conversation goes between the you who is rational and the you who has been hurt. The cycle of defeat never ends.

Why not talk about it to the One who really loves you and who lets you know it like no other. . .

O, Father, there are so many times when I feel unlovable . . . so very small . . . so unworthy of anything. I see others who seem vibrant, confident, and secure . . . and I want to run and hide in a dark place. But I remember that You love me . . . that I am important to You. How I thank you for knowing the depths of me . . . the part of me no one else knows . . . and for loving me just the same. . .

> *You have searched me and known me . . . You understand my thoughts. . .*
> *You are intimately familiar with everything about me. . .*
> *You have surrounded me with Yourself . . . You have Your hand upon me.*
> *I will always be within Your presence . . . wherever I go . . .*
> *I will be held by Your right hand. . .*

I will have Your light for my darkness.
You created me to be the way I am...
to live my life within Your frame of time...
according to Your own planning from long, long ago.
You are always with me ... whether I am awake or
asleep...
I am priceless to You ... I am dearly loved.

"I have loved you with an everlasting love; I have drawn you with loving kindness."

(Jeremiah 31:3)

REFLECTIONS

_____

_____

_____

_____

_____

_____

_____

_____

_____

_____

RESISTANCE TO CHANGE

Change! If there is anything hard for you to deal with, it is change. It seems as if there have already been more changes than you thought possible.

You have changed.

Your relationships have changed . . . or at least are in the process of changing.

The rules of life have changed as you have assumed responsibility for your feelings.

And, in reality, you have adjusted fairly well.

You have managed to function, to keep on keeping on despite the fact that your world has seemed to be at a full tilt for so long.

But now, the latest change seems threatening . . . just too much . . . and everyone is watching to see how "well" you are as you grapple to maintain your balance.

The Lord knows and understands how fragile you feel . . . how unnerved and off balance. He invites you to take time to come to Him and cling tightly to all that He is.

O Father, I don't understand what is happening . . . my world is turning upside down . . . I feel the turmoil . . . I want to run away . . . I want to escape whatever this is . . . I don't know who I am or where I am going . . .

But You say that You are in control . . . I choose to believe You . . . and that is enough.

Thank you that You rule over all . . . that Your eyes run to and fro through the whole earth seeking someone whose heart is completely Yours . . .

Thank you that You do according to Your will in the host of heaven and among the inhabitants of the earth . . . and no one can stand against You.

Thank you that nothing is hidden from Your sight, but all things are open to Your eyes . . .

*Thank you that all Your ways are righteous and holy
... and that You are causing all things to work
together for good in my life...
Thank you that I can always give thanks to You in all
things ... even when I don't understand...*

"Let the beloved of the Lord rest secure in him, for he shields him all day long, and the one the Lord loves rests between his shoulders."

(Deuteronomy 33:12)

"Yours, O Lord, is the greatness and the power and the glory and the majesty and the splendor, for everything in heaven and earth is yours. Yours, O Lord, is the kingdom; you are exalted as head over all."

(1 Chronicles 29:11–12)

REFLECTIONS

_____

_____

_____

_____

_____

_____

_____

_____

_____

BROKENNESS

There it is again. Someone is talking about brokenness. The eternal reminder is there. "It is the crushed grape that yields the wine." It sounds so logical, so antiseptic, so natural. But no one ever mentions the flies and the yellow jackets that swarm around the lifeless skins of crushed grapes. No one ever talks about the sour stench that invades the air. No one ever mentions that the splitting of the grape skin is agonizing. No one ever says that brokenness hurts.

You look at what God says. There is no doubt that brokenness is a necessary state for the believer. You look closer and see that God says it will hurt . . . that it will come only through fiery trials. He doesn't pull any punches.

But brokenness for you has come in such a strange form. God says, "Don't be surprised at the fiery ordeal." But in all your caring and trusting, you never thought your fiery ordeal would take place in this relationship.

You never dreamed that brokenness before God would come from a heart broken by "the other."

Jesus Christ came to heal your broken heart. Those may only be words to you right now . . . but the Father longs to make them reality in your heart. "God mends the broken heart when you give Him all the pieces."

The words of the songs swirl in my mind . . ." Can that which is broken ever be mended again?" . . . "Where do broken hearts go?" . . . and on and on. . .

Father, I feel bruised and broken. My thoughts are shadowy . . . cloudy . . . vague. I can't seem to sort them out, put them in place, understand them. I feel weak and fragile . . . I'm crumbling inside.

Thank you, Father, for being here with me. You are the mender of broken hearts . . . broken relationships . . . broken lives. You give me hope. You will give me the strength to begin

again . . . the wisdom to know how. Thank you that You are my
healer and sustainer and that I can rest in You.

"He sent His word and healed them, and delivered them from their destructions."

(Psalm 107:20 NASB)

"Heal me, O Lord, and I will be healed; save me and I will be saved, for you are the one I praise."

(Jeremiah 17:14)

REFLECTIONS

UNCONTROLLED THOUGHTS

You have heard it again and again. "Whatever is true, whatever is honorable, whatever is right, whatever is pure, whatever is lovely, whatever is of good repute, if there is any excellence and if anything worthy of praise, let your mind dwell on these things."

That is your goal. That's what you want to do, what you know you must do . . . but when you least expect it, the memory comes quietly drifting through . . . distracting . . . distressing . . . depressing. You think your guard is strong. After all, it has been so long ago. But when the thoughts come, they are as fresh as yesterday, as compelling as today.

You don't want them. You don't want to relive that era in your mind. But in a moment you can be transported with all the vivid emotions that time in your life conjures up.

Could you be under the control of something as intangible as a thought? Are you helpless in the grip of phantom memories? Surely not. But if not, then what is going on?

You may never answer your own questions, but you have a God who says you are "fearfully and wonderfully made." He created your mind and He understands every intricate detail of thought patterns and imaginations. Your questions belong to Him.

O Father, I'm not sure how it started. It came through a glance . . . or was it a tone of voice . . . triggering thoughts of painful words spoken in the past. One thought led to another . . . and then another, bringing deep-seated feelings which overwhelmed me. Before I realized it, there was a battle in my mind.

I reasoned . . . it was over. It was another time . . . another place . . . another person. Over. Why should I care? What difference does it make now anyway? Still . . . my emotions plummeted. The battle raged on. I felt the depths of depression . . . the agony of rejection . . . torn apart. I was being defeated . . . I was losing the battle in my mind.

Until . . . I remembered. Your Spirit, who calls all things to our remembrance (John 14:26), spoke quietly to my heart and reminded me. . .

"Thou wilt keep him in perfect peace, whose mind is stayed on thee: because he trusteth in thee."

(Isaiah 26:3 KJV)

"Do not be anxious about anything, but in everything, by prayer and petition, with thanksgiving, present your requests to God. And the peace of God, which transcends all understanding, will guard your hearts and your minds in Christ Jesus."

(Philippians 4:6–7)

Thank you, O Father, for showing me how to have peace of mind by focusing my thoughts on You and Your truths. Thank you that You have shown me how to think biblically, how to turn my worries over to You, and how to refuse thoughts that would only bring me down. I pray that You will help me to recognize the reflections, the suggestions, and the reminders which start the downward spiraling of my emotions as they so subtly overtake me . . . that I might bring them in line with Your truths and win the battle in my mind.

REFLECTIONS

A NEGATIVE SELF-IMAGE

People all around you give you compliments, but you can't seem to grasp what they say. Their words don't quite reach your heart. Nothing penetrates. Nothing stays long enough to be considered.

All you can see is you don't measure up. You're not what others think you are and if they knew the truth about you ... if they really knew you ... they wouldn't think you measure up either.

Your greatest fear is someone getting to know you and not liking you any more. They will discover the incompetence you know is there beneath your facade of "being so capable." You hate that feeling, but more than anything, you hate to let anyone know who you really are. You try to keep to yourself, but it seems someone is always trying to pry. Someone is always trying to get to know the "real you."

You hate to get up in the morning because today may be the day "they" find out who you really are. Being exposed for who you think you really are is the worse case scenario. When you don't like yourself why should anyone else like you.

The Lord knows your fear and He longs to hear from you. . . . He longs to comfort you and show you who you really are in Him.

O Lord ... morning has come. The sun is shining ... the air is clear ... the day ahead is full of hope. But...

Fear clouds my hope. I fear failure ... fear the reproach of others ... fear I am not good enough ... fear who I am.

Who am I? I am Your child, redeemed by Your blood, forgiven because of the price You paid. I am a new creation in You, saved and kept by Your grace, loved with Your everlasting, unfailing, and unconditional love ... just because You want to love me.

Thank you that You...

    ... have begun a good work in me and will complete it.

    ... are working in me to will and to do Your good purpose.

    ... are molding me and making me into the person You created me to be ... like You.

I am God's gift. I will remember that. I will walk in the light of who I am.

"Being confident of this, that he who began a good work in you will carry it on to completion until the day of Christ Jesus."

(Philippians 1:6)

"I pray for them. I am not praying for the world, but for those you have given me, for they are yours."

(John 17:9)

REFLECTIONS

_____

_____

_____

_____

_____

_____

_____

_____

A TEMPTATION TO BLAME OTHERS

It is so hard for you to believe that you are actually responsible for how you feel. How many times did you think, feel, and say to "the other," "You make me so...." "You make me so happy." "You make me so mad." "You make me so anxious"... and on and on the "You make me sOs" were traded between you. Then one day you woke up and began to take responsibility for what you did, what you said, how you felt ... and things began to change. Responsibility severed the thin thread holding your relationship together.

When you decided to assume responsibility, it meant you had to speak the truth, whether he became angry or not, and often he was angry. It meant you had to act like an adult, with no childlike excuses. Responsibility was to learn, even harder to put into practice. The cost was high and there have been times you wondered if it was worth it. But you have grown to see that for a Christian, there are no alternatives for assuming responsibility.

When you struggle, take time to talk it over with Your Lord.

As my life moves further away from the relationship which was once so close to my heart, one which filled so much of my thoughts and time, You show it to me in a different light, Father. As time goes on, old feelings dim, intensity fades. You are healing my heart.

Now I can see my responsibility a little clearer ... though maybe not yet as clear as it will someday become. I can see the error in my anger ... in the manipulations ... in the possessiveness ... in allowing myself to become someone I never thought I'd be ... in allowing it to continue.

I realize, Father, that no one can...
   ... make me do what I don't want to do
   ... control my feelings
   ... use me ... unless I allow it.

I alone am responsible for...

. . . what I think
. . . how I feel
. . . how I respond

I know that, through You, I can have. . .
. . . love, joy, peace
. . . acceptance
. . . value and self-worth.

Thank you, Lord, for showing me that I must take responsibility for my life . . . that You do not accept my blaming others for how I think and act. Thank you for teaching me, through Your Word, that I can think right thoughts . . . which will cause me to have right feelings . . . which will cause me to behave in ways which honor You. I cannot hold anyone else responsible for me. I will be responsible.

REFLECTIONS

_____

_____

_____

_____

_____

_____

_____

_____

_____

PLEASE REMIND ME....

Recovering from codependency can best be compared to recovery from surgery. The process is slow and excruciatingly painful at first, but with each passing day you will gain new strength and the pain will lessen.

If you are going to heal successfully, your recovery period is critical. You have gone through a lot, so don't expect yourself to be in working order immediately. Give yourself time to heal, but don't allow yourself a moment for self-pity. You have been given everything you need to get better and to do it gracefully. God has said if you are His child, you have "everything you need for life and godliness." Remember the aim of your recovery is to be able to live life as God intended it to be lived.

As you have reflected on each emotion that accompanies recovery from codependency, no doubt you have experienced a wide spectrum of feelings that at times overwhelmed you. Because they often appear when you least expect them, those feelings can be frightening and defeating. Just about the time you believe you are getting better, you can have a relapse that takes you by surprise. Remember, dear friend, it is not injurious to experience a relapse of intense emotion. The damage is done if you choose to allow these feelings to reclaim control of your thinking and behavior. The big set-backs can come if you allow yourself to drift into your old comfort zone of wrong thinking and behaving. It can be deadly to your emotional health and you know it, but in a moment of weakness you may be tempted to give into some of your old responses.

Whenever this occurs, it is an extremely critical time. It is at this point in your recovery that you must assume responsibility. You must recognize that you are being drawn back into unhealthy dependencies. To fail to assume responsibility by taking control of your emotional health is to send yourself right back into surgery or worse, to allow the battle with codependency to overtake you again. If you really want to get better and stay healthy, we encourage you to seriously consider these reminders as you continue on your journey toward wholeness.

Be Willing To Recognize Your Problem with Codependency.

Denial is never healthy. To accept the problem and to be honest with yourself is a major step toward healing. You don't have to wear the label of "codependent." You just need to recognize that you are susceptible to the enticements that codependency seems to offer.

Be Willing To Admit to Yourself When You Are Being Drawn Back to Codependent Behavior.

If in doubt, ask yourself, "Will what I want to do create freedom of bondage? Will it make me and 'the other' more responsible or will it cause either of us to revert to irresponsible, hurtful behavior."

Be Willing To Develop Other Interests.

Too much attention on one person promotes unhealthy dependency. Several good relationships in various areas of your life will be healthier emotionally, will make your life more interesting, and will give you a broader, more objective outlook.

Be Willing To Assume Responsibility To Transfer Your Dependency from the Other Person to God.

This will require an intense effort to discover for yourself the character and attributes of God. Until you learn to trust Him, you will be limited in your ability to depend on Him. It is our human nature to trust in the known rather than the unknown.

Be Willing To Deal Biblically with the Intense Feelings You Have Been Experiencing.

The Scriptures are filled with guidelines for behavior that is acceptable to God and will bring peace and freedom with man.

Intense emotions cloud objectivity. The Scriptures will give you the objectivity you are lacking.

Be Willing To Watch Out for the Rebound.

When you have successfully exited one codependency, you are still an emotional being who can be hooked by the right person in the right situation. Listen to those around you whom you trust and love. If someone new comes into your world, don't be too quick to rush into a close relationship. Remember, your objectivity is not always clear.

Be Willing To Set Aside Your Identification as a Victim.

Too often recovering codependents slow their own healing process by hanging onto a victim mentality. If you see yourself as a victim, then you will act like a victim. Such behavior invites victimization. Remember, you are the servant of God, not the victim of men.

Be Willing To Persevere.

Healing is worth the time, the pain, and the effort. Remember, you do have a choice. When you are tempted to fall back to your old, codependent ways of behaving, consider your options. You can either make the effort to discipline yourself to think and act in the healthy way you have learned, or you can let yourself slip into the old, unhealthy ways of relating. Both choices involve pain, but you will always be unstable if you fail to persevere in your journey.

Be Willing To Get Back Up When You Fall.

Falling is not failure and it is not the end of the world. If you slip into your old patterns or even if you all headlong into another codependent relationship, you can get up and start again. It is never too late. There is always hope.

Be Willing To Keep a Journal.

Keeping a record of your feelings and responses will help you see how far you have come. It will also give you insight into the situations that are likely to give you problems.

Be Willing To Begin Today.

Procrastination will only leave you feeling defeated and increasingly out of control. Your journey begins when you decide that you will dare to take the first step.

Remember, you are a valued and loved person. God longs to relate to you as your Father, your Friend, and your Companion for life. He offers healing and wholeness no matter how broken you may feel. He is the One who has plans for you . . . plans for a future and a hope, no matter how far you have fallen.

Perhaps you have always longed to have a personal relationship with Him and yet the prayers and the promises always seem to be for someone else. If that is where you are in your journey, then you can find the answers for your questions and the fulfillment for your longings. And it can all begin today as you make the decision to give all you know of you to all you know of the God who created you, who can heal your hurts, and who has the answer for your life. The place to begin your journey is on your knees, as you recognize your own helplessness and your need for a savior.

You might want to pray a prayer and just tell Him how you feel. Remember, it's not the words you say, but the motive of your heart. God says that He is near to the brokenhearted. You may want to say something like this:

> God, I know that I can't run my own life. My natural ways are away from You. I feel empty and broken but I want to live the way You want me to live. So I am giving all I know of me to all I know of You. I ask You to come into my life and take control of me. I know that You can do this because You created me and You came to this earth as the Lord Jesus Christ to save me—to die and pay the penalty for my sins, so that I can have eternal life. I accept the free gift of Your salvation. Thank you for loving me, for saving me, and for the new life You have given me. Amen.

Precious, precious friend, if you still have questions about what it means to become a child of God, we invite you to turn to the Appendix and read, asking God to lead you into all truth. God has promised, "If you seek for me, you will find me."

We want to encourage you to use this book of reflections as a gentle reminder that you are in the process of healing. You may not be where you want to be, but you have come a long way from where you were. Remember this: You will get better. It will take time. There is hope.

APPENDIX

HOW CAN I BECOME A CHRISTIAN?

1. What does it mean to be a Christian?

To be a Christian is to have a relationship with Christ. It is spoken of as being saved, being born again.

Being saved refers to salvation from the penalty of sin by entering into a personal relationship with Jesus Christ. It means that you can live victoriously during this lifetime and go to heaven when you die.

Being born again refers to a spiritual rebirth that takes place when you acknowledge sin in your life, repent (agree with God about sin), accept Jesus Christ's payment for sin, and commit your life to Him. To be born again is to be saved, to have salvation, to be a Christian.

2. What is sin?

Failure to meet God's standards
Doing your own thing
Having your own way
Disobeying God in thought, word, or deed
"And we like sheep have gone astray, we have turned every one to his own way. . . ." (Isaiah 53:6).

3. Who are sinners? Aren't most people basically good? Everyone has sinned.

". . . all have sinned and are falling short of the honor and glory which God bestows and receives" (Romans 3:23).

"For the wages which sin pays is death; but the (bountiful) free gift of God is eternal life through (in union with) Jesus Christ, our Lord" (Romans 6:23).

4. Why is sin so bad?

Sin separates you from God.

"But your iniquities have made a separation between you and your God, and your sins have hid His face from you, so that He will not hear" (Isaiah 59:21).

5. Since sin has separated me from God, is there any hope?

Yes. God has done everything necessary to provide a way for your salvation.

"For God so greatly loved and dearly prized the world that He (even) gave up His only-begotten Son, so that whosoever believes in (trusts, clings to, relies on) Him shall not perish—come to destruction, be lost—but have eternal (everlasting) life" (John 3:16).

6. How did Jesus provide salvation?

His death on the cross paid for sin. He accepted the penalty for your sin and paid the price.

"But He was wounded for our transgressions, He was bruised for our guilt and iniquities; the chastisement needful to obtain peace and well-being for us was upon Him, and with the stripes that wounded Him we are healed and made whole" (Isaiah 50:5).

7. How can I be saved?

By entering into a personal relationship with Jesus Christ through trusting in (believing in, having faith in) Him and His payment for sin. You must believe that....

"... Christ, the Messiah, the Anointed One, died for our sins in accordance with (what) the Scriptures (foretold)."
"That He was buried, that He arose on the third day as the Scriptures foretold" (1 Corinthians 15:3–4).

8. What will happen when I do this?

Your sins will be forgiven. And, because your sins are forgiven, they will no longer separate you from God.

"In Him we have redemption (deliverance and salvation) through His blood, the remission (forgiveness) of our offenses (shortcomings and trespasses), in accordance with the riches and generosity of His gracious favor. . . ." (Ephesians 1:7).

You will be sealed with the Holy Spirit of God.

"In Him you also who have heard the Word of Truth, the glad tidings (gospel) of your salvation, and have believed in and have adhered to and have relied on Him, were stamped with the seal of the long-promised Holy Spirit" (Ephesians 1:13).

You will have eternal life.

"He who possesses the Son has life; he who does not possess the Son of God does not have that life" (1 John 5:12).

9. I do want to be saved. How do I do it?

Talk to God. Tell Him how you feel. You might say something like this:

"God, I know that I have sinned—in thought, word, and deed. I have lived for myself and not for you. Thank you for sending Jesus to pay for my sin by giving His life on the cross. I want Jesus to come into my heart and be my Savior."

10. Must I do anything else?

Tell others about your decision to be a Christian.

"Because if you acknowledge and confess with your lips that Jesus is Lord and in your heart believe (adhere to, trust in, and rely on the Truth) that God raised Him from the dead, you will be saved" (Romans 10:9).

Now that you are a Christian, you are a part of the family of God (John 1:12) and you can never lose that position. You have been reborn, and 2 Corinthians says this about you:

"Therefore, if any person is (ingrafted) in Christ, the Messiah, he is (a new creature altogether) a new creation; the old (previous moral and spiritual condition) has passed away. Behold, the fresh and new has come!"

11. How does being a Christian, being born again, change a person who is emotionally dependent?

Jesus Christ is now in His rightful position in your life. He has become your master, owner, friend, and companion for life. The Holy Spirit lives within you and gives you power to live in obedience to God. You now have the power not to sin. Since He still gives you a free will, the choice is under your control. He simply enables you to make a choice.

As you prayerfully read and meditate upon Scripture, saturating your mind with God's Word, He will transform your life (Romans 12:2). As you begin to know Him as the faithful, loyal, trustworthy, loving Savior, you will realize He is the only One who can truthfully say, "I will never leave you nor forsake you." He alone is worthy of your total dependence. His greatest desire is to have a relationship with you, and to have you take Him at His Word.